For Jdy —

So good to meet you . . .

Here's to the next best word

(expletive or not!)

in the best

order . . .

/Kevin

Self-
Portrait
With
Expletives

Cal Poly   9/18/13

KEVIN CLARK

Kevin Clark (signature)

Self-Portrait With Expletives

Lena-Miles Wever Todd Poetry Series / Pleiades Press

Rock Hill, South Carolina & Warrensburg, Missouri

ISBN 978-0-8071-3645-4

Published by Pleiades Press
Department of English & Philosophy
The University of Central Missouri
Warrensburg, Missouri 64093
&
Department of English
Winthrop University
Rock Hill, South Carolina 29733

Distributed by Louisiana State University Press

Cover Image: *Deus Ex Machina (Hanging Man)* © by Brian O'Connor
Book design by Kevin Prufer. Author's photo © by Dennis Steers.

2 4 6 8 9 7 5 3 1
First Pleiades Press Printing, 2010

Thanks to the editors of the following journals: *American Literary Review* (Radio Fate), *Artful Dodge* (Scrim), *Askew* (Self-Portrait with Expletives), *Confrontation* (I'm Fine), *Crazyhorse* (Approaching Days), *Eclipse* (Sixties Noir), *The Georgia Review* (The Bedspread at Echo Lake, "Le Secret"), *The Greensboro Review* ("Whipping Post"), *Gulf Coast* (Six Miles Up), *The Iowa Review* (James Dickey at Florida), *Kestrel* (Flashback at Castlefranco), *Literal Latte* (Poem Written in Panic and Hope...), *The Marlboro Review* (This Morning), *The Notre Dame Review* (Eight Hours in the Nixon Era), *Ploughshares* (This, Then), *RATTLE* (Class Politics), *Solo Café* (Accident Alert), and *The Wallace Stevens Review* (Solstice over the Valdarno). "The Boat" appears in the anthology *Where Icarus Falls*. "Eight Hours in the Nixon Era" is re-printed in the anthology *The Notre Dame Review: The First Ten Years*.

I'm gratified by the generous assistance of so many people: At The Bolinas Salon: Wendy Barker and Hannah Stein. In San Luis Obispo: Lisa Coffman, James Cushing, John Hampsey, Mary Kay Harrington, Ginger Adcock Hendrix, Al Landwehr, and Todd James Pierce. In the wide world: Ralph Black, Martha Collins, Brad Comann, Stephen Corey, Denise Duhamel, David Kirby, Susan Ludvigson, Kevin Prufer, and David St. John. Thanks as well to all my students everywhere from whom I continue to learn. And thanks to Cal Poly, the College of Liberal Arts and the English Department for granting a sabbatical. I'm grateful, too, for the support of my colleagues Stan Rubin, Judith Kitchen, and the rest of the faculty at the Rainier Writing Workshop in Tacoma. Thanks also to my aunt, Mary Higgins Clark, for a lifetime of encouragement. And, as ever, my most enduring love for and gratitude to my wife, Amy Hewes.

NATIONAL
ENDOWMENT
FOR THE ARTS

Financial Assistance for this project has been provided by the Missouri Arts Council, a state agency, and the National Endowment for the Arts.

MISSOURI ARTS COUNCIL

for Joe and Hannah

Contents

Six Miles Up

As if what's said here is not my heart's wreck.
As if turbulence did not author the need.
As if this scribbling were not last counsel.
As if this sheet would be found in the breach.

As if you, son, were reading this fifty years from now.
As if you held it in your hands like a violin.
As if you would listen for the secrets.
As if the music of the blue altitude signified.

As if you, daughter, bequeathed this poem to your daughter.
As if on her first day of adulthood she read and knew.
As if from this vantage I held love for her.
As if my love were actual atoms.

As if this letter did not enter the crematorium of the attic.
As if it did.

1

Eight Hours in the Nixon Era

The parabola of the suitcase as it flew
    from the Watergate balcony mimicked
my inner life the year the low voice
    on the phone said, FBI, do you know
a Bob Grant? My mother, a Republican

County Supervisor, was at church.
    It was a complex era. Did we laugh
too easily? Was I to tell the agent
    that Bob was a friend who'd palmed
a credit card for a wild DC ride

as Sam Irvin and the good guys were
    moving in for the kill? Bob, whose jet south
would pass DC-bound Air Force One
    that midnight, November 18th, 1973,
just after Nixon claimed he was no crook.

Bob had invited me for the gig, but
    I knew better—and I didn't know better
often. Bob seduced Ralph and Jenny,
    both staying the month in Jersey with me
and my publicity-conscious mother,

the same Ralph and Jenny who were on
    the verge of dissolution, ever since
I'd been falling for Jenny and she for me,
    though of course Ralph was my best friend,
and Jenny and I hated ourselves, hippie

clichés sloughing into a closet or basement.
　　　Even now I try to laugh it off. I told
Agent Kaplaw I'd never heard of Bob
　　　Grant. Boozy Bob, with whom I'd smoked
weed for six years in college while his muddy

Utah speakers alternately shook from
　　　Zeppelin sex riffs and Streisand show tunes,
who we later discovered longed himself
　　　to sleep with Ralph, *that* Bob had only
minutes earlier answered the suite phone,

hung up, looked at Ralph and Jenny with
　　　the gravity of a guy on bad acid, all
of them wordlessly putting into effect
　　　Escape Plan A, Ralph heading to the car
while Jenny and Bob packed the one suitcase

with the contraband of a good DC shopping
　　　blitz, compliments of a Mr. Robert Kitchen,
address at this point unknown, owner
　　　of a missing gold MasterCard. I hung up.
My mother pulled in the drive. The phone

didn't ring. It continued not to ring.
　　　As Ralph pulled to the curb and Bob and
Jenny descended down the elevator,
　　　exited, then stuffed the goods back
in the split suitcase and jumped into

the Cutlass, also rented courtesy of
　　　Mr. Kitchen, and headed for Dulles,
my mother and I chatted about Mass
　　　and Father Mulroney's somnambulant
sermon, though she didn't care to knock

the priest because she still harbored
     hope that my rejection of the family faith
was a temporary moral seizure and didn't
     want to sour the wine while I lapsed.
She went upstairs for her afternoon nap.

The phone rang. Agent Kaplaw assured me
     he would slap a warrant on my ass
for aiding and abetting and haul me down
     to DC if I didn't talk. I gave up Bob,
then hung up. Do we laugh too easily?

My mother's hero the President
     was a traitor—nothing else
to call it. He'd lost her faith. And how
     could she win
next year's election? Car doors slammed

in front of the house. I met Ralph and Jenny
     outside. One look at me and they knew
trouble had trailed them. We called Bob
     at home in Gainesville. He would
turn himself in, as he'd promised. We

told my mother that rich Bob wasn't
     so rich as he'd made out, that he'd urged
Ralph and Jenny to DC for a weekend
     on him, that the weekend was stolen,
that the FBI had traced the billed calls

to *her* house. So practiced, we lied
     to soften the story, but
she had a Republican fit anyway.
     Soon enough Ralph left for California,
Jenny and I took a house, taught GED

in Jersey, Bob called the president
        of MasterCard and worked off
the three grand. No jail time. It's still
        a complex era, how the comic
can shroud regret. Jenny and I hit the road

for California, then broke up six years later
        when she became a Rolfer,
a Gestalt therapist, went in for enema
        and past lives therapies—
separately, I think. Bob is gay in Florida,

Ralph slept with another friend's lover,
        and now he's married to her.
I'm married, too, happy and faithful
        for two decades. In the adrenaline rush
of time, Ralph and I have remained

best of friends. We try to navigate
        all the old stories. When
our families vacation together, suitcases
        bloat, rarely fly.
I sometimes think of Nixon, how he failed us all.

Sixties Noir

Smoke means cash, said the stoned collector.
Codie laughed, then paid
The toll with hash. We'd loaned
Ourselves each other, rode
Windowpane down the Jersey summer,
Her face gone jumpin jack flash,
Her crossroads aura
Sheer as her peasant blouse.

As she twirled the spliff in flame,
I blinked away
The bearded infant narcs
Winking from the starboard wing of the Impala.

By Wildwood, both of us loved
The life we'd worn.
On the starry beach, new friends
Riffed in whispers,
Knew never to Bogart.

Heading home, her same smile
And the turnpike smog
Layered lacquer on my heart. Then,
Visions redux: Altar boys on bennies
Sang the Sanctus in double time.
Cops roved the rearview.
Straight as a line, I couldn't stop
Hallucinating. We drove
The surface roads, said we'd never pay a cent.

Codie held to the wheel, dropped me in Hackensack.
I cracked for good, then headed west.

James Dickey at Florida

1973

PERFORMANCE

The first time I saw James Dickey
He stood at the head of the class, unzipped
His wetsuit jacket, then announced
In surplus Buckhead slur,
You don't fuck around with poetry.
Don Armstrong smiled so still

No one saw him. Bridget's perm sank.
When you're masturbating, he said,
There's that feeling just before you come…
—*That's* poetry. Donna's lovely fingers
Twirled still beneath her throat.
You'd think my history of bad acid

Would have readied me, but
I too churned in the vortex. Before
Deliverance, he'd been teaching
At Bread Loaf where Auden had only
Five students. Wystan, ol' friend,
He asked, How is it you have so few

And I so many? Auden told him
He'd ask a simple question, then dismiss
Those who answered wrong.
—Now he'd ask us the same:
Why do you write poetry?
I fell and froze. Two weeks back

I'd read Auden's Q-and-A.
—I'm born to. —I have something to say.
—It's in the blood. Down the row
They came, each wrong answer
Stung by the clipped dismissal:
You'd be out of the class. *You'd* be out. *You.*

Do I give the right response and blow
His cover? As if miraculous light
Poured up from the lacquered desk
To save me, he nodded past my chair.
Soon, someone hemmed
Auden's dull trimeter:

I like to play with words.
Then, without warning, he staged
A battle of accents. First
The movie's cracker sheriff
Barks *he'd* written "Dueling Banjos."
Then Brando's puffed Don Vito throats:

I said, You don't fuck around with poetry.
That's when the dueling personas
Waged a litany of suicidal proofs:
Thomas is gone. Jarrell is gone.
Roethke is gone. Plath. Berryman.
A pause came on like bourbon—

And as the last lean trick amazed us,
Armstrong's seat sat empty:
Lowell, he said, will be the next to go.
—Shadows shimmered in the margins,
But we hung rapt still. Quiet
Bled us pale. One after another,

He gripped us each in a long scowl,
Then dropped his gaze toward
The waxed, fluorescent grave
Of the seminar room. I rode
My heart down a sink hole.
He walked out, left himself for dead.

ENGINE

Weeks later   backlit by The Millhopper's bar lights   Bridget's floating hair
As promise and aesthetic   our second beer entering the veins
Of her story: how the giant poet pulled her without shame to the pool table
Bourbon no water no lyric just fame   how he asked her quick like that
And when she laughed him off in the first neon mist of thinking
This is a comic ride he's joking   he turned without ceremony
To the grad student from Psych   then the blonde bartender   then
Donna sitting with her professor boyfriend   when at last he hulked alone
To a barstool, reciting stories to the mirror until he rose
And the door opened for his dark walk home   Bridget said his grip
Locked her arm with such soft metal   amazing focus, she said,
Elemental   —Detached, corrected Donna   —A pilot, I'm thinking now,
Trying to outclimb the flak   the concussive strobe   the will to rise
Above an illimitable sky   I'd wanted the mysteries the poems

The sex Bridget's breath in my hair   not just the life, but
The orbital star-strewn realm to which each line aspires   that year
I mimicked his fast, hunter's yawp   But in truth I'd dreamed a different
Romance   a woman as conduit and twin   the complementary vocable
That completes the code   moves the aerie gears of the last lock
Until we've crossed past bliss itself into the weightless lyric union
At the heart of poetry   —Didn't we all?   Even those young professors
Of the South   married before the hallucinatory countercultural acids
Had bleached away the iambs the dates the seven ambiguities   the cramped
Hieroglyphs scrawled over their fugitive drafts   each premature father
On a track I'd come to hope for   all lined up against the back wall
Of the class three weeks later   drawn to spectacle   to history

And region   When in a brooding globe of spirits the poet hauled himself
Into his seat before the dark-haired visitor   not gravitas but hell-to-pay
In his eyes   on his right hand an oversized turquoise Thunderbird ring—
He never looked at his mistress from the Carolinas, his "secretary"
Handing out our copied poems, a thin smile bobbing its incessant Yes
Donna's broken music first   her sweet-dreams mimicry of Mr. Henry's songs
Undoing the poet whose mouth curled and snapped its No   then snarled
How bad this first line read—   And even then   before the primacy
Of what's-to-come   you could see in his face   the right engine sputter
The words fail   then: the maw opened like a hole in the sky   Then:
We heard the woman speak into the silence   Oh, she doesn't know,
She thinks it's a good line   and how the poet turned to stare a bare
Half second   How the right hand lifted   how the woman's cheek
Went white then purpled after the backhand struck—   I can still track

His hand   its open caesura   the quick mid-flight hesitation   in the old
Parlance, he'd pulled his punch—   a poem twisting nose-down
In freefall each flexed line gone flaccid   the old oceanic sky breaking
Open like cowardice   —or the last silk shreds   of what's right
Snapped off at last….

                    He spun Donna's poem to the floor, said
He didn't want to do more *student* poetry—   the dark-haired woman
Quiet as a grave, eyes brimming, a bird rising in red on her face—
When a grad student in Lit handed him an open book   asked if he'd read
One of his poems   and so   He looked down upon the story
Of the young man who leaves his motorcycle roadside   convoys
Through the junkyard to some grandmother's Pierce Arrow—
While stunned and shot we actually listened   not one of us had risen
In protest—   The narrator held and held to Doris Holbrook
With terrific speed   the poet's voice as taut as the string-triggered 12-gauge
The girl's father held in wait for him—   that gun compelling
The sort of lust that drives a boy like this   who soon leaves Doris Holbrook
As she scrambles with car parts back to her old man…   To this day
I can hear the poet's throat scratching its pitch-perfect rasp toward closure,
The boy on his engine   the poet wild to be wreckage he's already become
—And the rest of us: virgin players   each desk edge scoring our bloodless hands.

Class Politics

1

It was clear Maurice had been messed with plenty—
and that he'd messed right back. At the second class,
I asked him a question about a Faulkner story,
and he sized me up with a look that said

you may be my age and my teacher, but
if you ever screw with me I'll guarantee
the DNA you've stored in your miserable balls
for that sweet-ass kid you're planning

will meet a death so horrible only dogs will hear
your screams. I'd never had a vet that burnt
in class before, but I knew to believe the look.
Semi-official word from on-high claimed

at least three released murderers had joined
the student body, and that day Maurice
brought this factoid into gut-check relief.
I'd already explained how each student gets

at least one question every class, but plainly he
wasn't impressed with my pedagogy, so I made sure
only to call on him when his face said it was okay
this time. Raw red skin between black strands

of beard, the irises of his eyes full open as if he saw
inside and out at once, he looked like burst flesh
willed back into a man.

2

Only one other

re-entry student took my class that term:
A criminology major, pretty dark-haired
middle-aged Angel from down-state Ohio
read every assignment with check-list zeal.

Each break she'd pull out a compact
for her midday mascara. She liked Frost,
she said, because he was just like her mother,
who, if you want to know, was hired on

as the first female cop in the county exactly
one year after her father died. The poet,
he seems all ladylike, she said. You know:
looks good sounds nice but down deep cuts no one

no slack, not like her two redneck sisters
who married way down the food chain and
didn't care their husbands roughed 'em up
every couple months. No one else spoke to Angel

outside of class—one girl said she was too weird
for wheels, a real nouveau bitch. But they liked
her stories, even if she talked over them all.
And since Maurice rarely spoke, the two hadn't

tangled.

3

A month into the term, he arrived
like a hit man at my office door—only to discuss
the upcoming essay he was writing on

Hemingway's "Big Two-Hearted River." All along
I'd wanted to ask him about his name, the kind
of crap even best friends must have put him
through. Then again, I wanted him to like me

well enough he'd never kill me, so with practiced
diffidence I asked what drew him to that story, and
he simply said, Nick had been to war. Turned out,
his paper was better than I'd have guessed, the writing

chopped into short, chewed sentences that linked
Nick's lonely, hip-booted fishing to the moment
Maurice shot up a hundred-yard line of bushes
from his boat on the Mekong, how he'd heard

the cries over the engine, but couldn't see who'd
been hit. That was it. Though he never wrote why Nick
pushed deeper into the thicket, he seemed
pleased enough with his "B."

4

Two weeks
before finals, the class squeezed into a circle
for Hurston's "Sweat." I asked them to imagine
Delia's life with her no-good husband Sykes

before he tried to kill her. Not a black kid
in the group, the usual talkers spoke up right away
with the kind of righteousness Hurston used
to condemn bony Delia into the four walls

of our own sins, how Delia remained outside the house
doing nothing while Sykes' mortal pleadings
poured from the windows. Twice I'd asked Angel
to screw down her urge to speak, at least so others

had time to answer questions. But this topic
just stripped her bolts of thread. That woman did
what she had to, she told the class with a clichéd,
uptempo sneer we'd not heard before. Haven't

you been in cities when those animals walk
full across the sidewalk and won't give you
the right of way? And in case we didn't catch
her meaning: Listen, she hummed, you gotta know,

those so-called *men*, they'd just as soon kill you
as rob you, then laugh as you're bleeding
there in the street. She paused, gave out
a last conclusive sigh. That's why they're called

niggers.

5

    Shot silent as the rest of the class,
ever a believer in their democratic right
to make ugly fools of themselves, I raced

through a brain full of broken lines. It was 1984,
and I felt that old teacherly urge to preserve
what we'd come to call "student dignity."
But I was also pressed to counter each word

she'd said, especially the last, going off
again and again in our ears. Angel sat back
without noticing the motionless air of the room,
her legs crossed in their black tailored slacks,

the pearl necklace, the earrings, the silver bracelet
all hung in place as if she were born to being right.
I was still looking at her

6

                         when I heard his voice.

At first, it came at me like static. I turned to see
Maurice speaking at the floor, then slowly raising
his face. When I turned back, Angel's eyes
began their slow-motion focus on him. It's not hard

to figure there're lots of different groups
in the world and none of them are all one way
or the other, he said, his low voice finding its way
through the brush. It's just a fact that

there are the ones you can tell right off
they're okay, and then there are some, he said,
—rotating his two-way gaze Angel's direction—
who are plain scum.

7

I can't remember

what I said. I know I stumbled a few seconds,
hyper conscious of the class, how we'd lost
any chance at that high when teacher and students
forget the other life, when only hours ago

an old boyfriend called in seductive apology,
or a wife to say she's ovulating, or
a drunk lieutenant to kill a few hours.
For a few seconds, all that's vanished. Decades

back, I expected transcendence every class. Pissed
at my own hesitation that day, I didn't realize
the students took home a story they'd tell for weeks.
I probably called it a class, then crawled back

to my office. Your students are the lesson,
was the zen motto. I doubt *they* felt I failed them.
Two weeks later I gazed up at Maurice
from the front desk as he handed me his final exam.

When I said goodbye, he looked me directly
in the eye, then simply nodded. I never saw him
again. Though he'd been the only student to scare
the wise-ass right out of me, I can still recall

the measured pitch of his voice that one moment,
as if he were talking to himself, even
as he stared right through Angel's stung face.
He was at war. She was not the enemy.

Self-Portrait with Expletives

—for Brian D'Arcy

I told Darse I planned on being a pacifist.
His lips cut half a grin, said I'd never get laid.
Girls will think you're queer, that's all.
It was high school, the suburban sixties.
What did we know? Twelve years later,
when he and I got run off a wet road
in early morning Ohio by some yahoos
in a pick-up rigged three stories high,
we were blitzing home to Jersey where
most natives stick for lack of options.
Where we came from, white kids
swore in the style of old paesanos,
a practiced underbite ratcheting
fast talk into glottal bonding.

***

So it was 6AM, we're pushing ninety
in a '75 Honda, pumped on gas station coffee,
talking women, how one after another
put us off till we both got laid by love
two years into college. Soon, we've caught
tail end of a minor transcendence:
a long-lost, sleep-deprived, high-pitched laugh
about some high school trick we'd pulled
on that douche bag Dave Bonacasta—
when, on a double-yellow no passing curve,
these tires high as our roof were singing madly
right goddam *there*, inches from Darse's head.
Turns out, the yahoos get their yucks
by leaning on the horn and cutting cars off
as they skimmed one-paint-layer close.
Darse pulled hard right when their one-ton

with those old dumbass sackbut horns
on the hood grazed our fender. We spun
like figure skaters, the "William Tell Overture"
dopplering past. I always wanted to be
the kind of guy who'd go macho-Buddhist-calm
in the nightmare screaming face of bad shit.
We'd been at a dead stop a good ten seconds
before quiet blew through us. Smiling Dave
used to say, Life's a shit sandwich—
each day you take another bite. Darse
sat back and smiled as if he were stoned
on angelic music. Me, I was a body
shivering at astral frequency
before I blew the third syllable
loud as a thrown rod: mu-ther-*fuck*-er.

***

At any dull moment, Darse could tap
his bottomless keg of rank words
and call me one of his thousand versions
of *skinny-assed pussy*—just to keep me
off guard. I figured there'd come an opening
to sucker-punch him into speechlessness
with a line just too orbital to take
without flinching. Clearly this would not
be that time. As he fishtailed after them,
I hoped his love of getting what's his
would be subverted to saving my ass.
I always loved Darse and his warrior smile.
He had a pre-violent stillness real tough guys
sensed legit. An old tight end who lived
to clothesline stunting linebackers—
an enforcer with an art degree who'd turn
union boss and live for big dick negotiating.
That moment in the two-lane high-speed AM,
I was voting for his recessive gene.

***

They lost us in the Midwest mist.
We figured they found our California plates
an offense against manliness... Soon
we pulled off that road into a diner
to stare through smoke at black coffee—
only to find the not-so-comic
chrome mouths of those sackbut horns
pulling in at us as we walked out of the diner
in a delusional calm. I knew by the crowbar
in the fat driver's hand that he'd recognized us
as unfriendlies. I also knew Darse liked
the way danger is a sudden tool
to tincture the air with that metallic scent
of purest oxygen. I think deep down
he even liked the two rednecks, as if
we were all intimates. The next two steps
we took seemed like virgin territory.
Fifteen patrons in the diner window
holding forks and coffee aloft as we decide
who makes the first asshole move.
Somebody asks somebody if he has
A goddamn problem. Somebody says,
Seems we do. Just then, a voice
of practiced boredom turns the four of us.
Henry, the officer is asking, you just off
the night shift? The patrons suck back
down into their nicotine lives. The fat guy
brings up a smile out of his gut, heads
into the diner, and the cop asks us
where we're heading, have a nice trip right away.

***

Dave swore he once saw the state border sign
read *Welcome to New Jersey. Fuck this shit.*
A mile past the Gap, Darse asked if I didn't think
we'd been pussies, just driving off like that.
I told him my wife loves the way I can talk
like a hood but admit to terminal pussiness.
And that gets you laid? he asked. That's
when I saw my opening. Listen, I said,
a friend just told me about a new idea
these Berkeley shrinks are floating, how
we're all born ready to fuck anyone,
from gay to straight and in between.
Darse just glowed like a Zen mobster.
Once more, I knew I couldn't rile him—
but I had to finish the loser rap. I told him
these philosopher shrinks say, down deep
we're always crying for the sex we won't do.
Darse said, that's one assholic theory—
then gunned past a Rheingold semi. You know,
I said, with half a Lodi look, Dave was right,
each day you take another bite. I watched
his palm cuff the wheel. Then Darse burned
a cool smile, his reply the sound of one hand
snapping: —Fuck me, he shrugged.

2

Radio Fate

I'm twelve and the Lafayette transistor
in its leather case is buried beneath
my pillow beneath my ear, my brother
asleep in the next bed, my mother down

the hall brushing her teeth, my beat father
cackling to himself as the monologue
finds the radios of the male northeast.
And while Jean Shepherd tells his story

about sad-assed peace-time Company K,
or how he led the improbable
Wanda Hickey to his only prom, or
how summer evenings his own bushed father

came home, sucked down a Windy City beer
and moaned at the rasping radio fate
of the White Sox, my father—who'd be dead
in two years—heaves an occasional

breathless laugh, and I begin to figure
how funny has to work. From 10:15
to 11, monologist Jean Shepherd
broadcast from The Limelight in the Village—

a brooding, otherworldly neon bar
in my Jersey picturing. Stories of the poor
luckless slobs in the masochistic grip
of what's-to-come showed each a searing

flash of success, led one regular guy
after another to the urgent verge
of garlands and a rejuvenate wife.
But then in Shepherd's voice-cracking

empathies they had to witness it all
dissolve in their calloused hands
as down deep they knew it would. Shepherd's
denouement led all of us to exhale

into the static. And as I heard my father
breathing tight above me to make sure
I'd turned off the radio, I'd heard
enough to know the future had to end

in tough luck, that if jokes held truth
I'd best be the butt of every wise-ass line
to come, that there was one darkness
only—and two ways to enter it.

Approaching Days

That night, my wife's face strobing afloat above me, rubber footsteps chirping
on linoleum, a syringe
blurred away on a chrome dish, I tried to hone in on the diagnosis
I'd been told
but hadn't heard. Her mouth worked a newly practiced script, her voice

swallowing the shrill tremor: *the kids with the neighbors, a clot in my lung.*
Behind her, cinderblocks morphed
from sage to Sixties pink: Each day's test tube of dark red spinal fluid
hung above my father's hospital bed
like a chronicle

of wounds: dark, light, lighter—
but then too dark again.
That's how they measured the aneuristic blood. That's how my young mother
read his worsening.
A week earlier, I'd listened

from feigned sleep
when the ambulance closed around him. Fourteen, I focused on his quick return,
though a new adult hum
prepped my bones for the worst. Finally, in the last days, she took me to him,
her hand steering me

through the hallways: Tapped awake, he found me into view, tried to work a smile.
I placed a book
on the table beside the strange blue flowers. The moment I noticed
the tubes, her eyes
sharpened upon me, exacted

my silence. I never saw him again. Now, it's deep night. A whispering
in the fluorescent provinces.
Air like ether. Broken breathing
above the near beds.
Pinprick LEDs

blinking in code. Over and over, my wife's face is forming words
in the air. Sometimes my son,
sometimes my daughter
offers a single question I can't understand, their voices snarled like roots.
A long way off, the doctors ask my mother

to leave the room. My father looks up at me, reads the approaching days
in my eyes. Morphine travels
my arm like an old excuse. My wife waves good-bye, as if no one
can save her, the kids.
My father sits up, holding my gift. He keeps reading

the same page, but can't remember the story. I reach to unclasp the book
from his fingers. Let me
read it for you, I say. But his eyes pan the room like a blind man's.
Hello? he searches.
I'm not here, I say.

I'm Fine

In the ER, Dr. Sue said my lung collapsed. But then, maybe it was fluid,
she tried. Maybe pneumonia. Like me, she was weighing the odds: Is this

the end of the line? Or a new start? Imagine a drill bit in your right side.
Imagine one tenth of a single breath, its sharp stop. Dr. Sue told my wife

a kidney may have metastasized into the right lung. I asked myself,
How can I make this work? Then I remembered! I was laid out

on a stretcher. Re-imagine the narrative, I told myself. Fluorescent lights
hummed a tune. Techs in blue smocks. My young dead father

floated in. His aneurism in all those poems. Just then, Dr. Vinnie hulked
above me, said maybe a blood clot lodged in a capillary. Nurse Ev

said Dr. Sue was on break, touched my wife at the elbow, asked
if she had "durable power of attorney." I pictured the summer sun

falling on ballplayers warming up only two blocks away. I had a game
tomorrow at six. Dr. Vinnie told me, don't worry, we'll have you

outta here soon. First, we'll test both legs for clots, then we'll give you
a new drug. Not FDA approved. But very, very good—prescribed all over

Europe. Who's to know what line will appear next? In walked a nurse
flicking a hypodermic. I tried a foot of trimeter: *Clot—Test—First*, I said.

She left forever. Then Dr. Jake showed up. He didn't seem to like Dr. Vinnie.
That's ok, I thought, they're good people, real pros. The ER floor gave off

its confident sheen. We're keepin' you here a week, just safer, he said.
Soon Nurse Antonia of lyric but indistinguishable descent gave me

morphine and I loved her as a mother. I closed my eyes to see
my two children. Then, for a full moment, I was dead. Each kid

was recovering with dignity, spoke elegies with restraint. Or so
everyone said. I let out a short, slow breath. A tech rolled in a computer

with octopus arms, said he was there to search the right leg for clots.
Both legs, I corrected. Maybe the poem *was* rounding into shape. He

went away and came back. Yes, sorry, *both* legs. The arms twirled
above my jellied groin. Nurse Antonia's second needle sent me

through the CT tunnel, my torso scanned in three-second slices. I slept
on outfield grass. Like that, Dr. Sue appeared. She too was tired, asked

how I felt. As my lips moved, the morphine played along, my poem living
the good life. I'm fine. Good, she said, good. Drs. Jake and Vinnie

have gone home to their wives. You can go home, too. No clots. Just
take this, a muscle relaxant. Turns out, she said with saintly release, you

pulled the trapezius in your back. Never heard of it, I said, then dozed
through a wheel chair ride. My wife lifted me into bed. There, the poem

took some time off. Mid-morning, the phone rang. Dr. Jake didn't ask,
How are you? Endings are always tough, and we were back

in the gut-check business. Return right now, he urged. We reviewed
the scan. Looks like a clot after all! I'm fine, I said. I'm on the way.

Poem written in panic and hope after reading Stephen Hawking's essay "Is Everything Determined?" in which he says, "Yes, it is, and here's why"

Say there's a chance he's wrong, that some

trans-dimensional pre-sub-atomic substance

sings its immaterial hosannas of pure meaning

from Out There to us, that the second proton

in a third orbit of the butterfly's right eye

is indelibly linked to the Shopping Network

on Sonic Boom Cable 12 by an invisible lyric

of moral connectives, some unified field theory

of non-particulate rays shooting from no single point

to my bagel toaster in a carrier wave too fine

to prove. As if Sister Teresa and Bishop Tutu

had frissoned away in a power spritz, crossing over

to channel a larger good through the instructive tubers

dangling invisible in the formulae of a string theory.

If he's wrong about the illimitable blankest space

between the latest discovered nano-quarks

of the Milky Way's caramel nucleus, about

the absent center of the ionic neo-cortex,

or the way each mad domino submits quietly

to knocking its neighbor in the dazzling

but irreversible clicks of the sequence, and

if he's wrong that we must click the cursor

on the laughing-man symbol at this very *now*, or that

in exactly thirty-seven hours and twenty-two minutes

Greenwich time on a sidewalk in a country

six-thousand relative and thus dismissable miles

from me, the brake must of course give

and an occupied wheelchair must begin its descent

down Ludgate Hill past the National Postal Museum

and on to St. Bartholomew's Hospital where wait

the scalpel and its bandages as ordained

even before the advent of the pteradactyl

or the shoehorn, then on a plainly sunlit morning

I may survey my dresser drawer profuse

with blue or tan socks, and pull my own choice

onto each foot like a guy with a plan, and walk

a king's walk through a land of lottery jingles

and love-struck nuns and real Hollywood drive-by's,

all of What's Next turned out just for me

like throngs of costumed subjects performing

their lives every day at The Festival of Accidents.

Solstice Over the Valdarno

that ambrosial latitude... —Stevens

Sunday solstice. Topmost sky awash in backlit blue,
then the blood-orange above the western ridge,
then the olive-black serration of hills—

and lower, the tiny lights of Figline
flickering on like breeze-blown candles
in the old cemetery in Florence—

                       and closest,
below our stone villa, a twine of smoke
above S. Michele, the late Renaissance church we visited
in sunlight as secular as the rented Renault
two days back. Now dusk, emergent
as another world I'd abandoned long ago.

                           Here at sunset
I'm joined by a voice unfurling beauty
from the sky and earth, from the long-dead
and my own nostalgia
              for Catholic endlessness—

***

As I sit among family, a constant query
whispers the terms of an argument.
                     Miles west
of our table of broken dolci and emptied cups
the sunset plays on for hours.
                Aunt Jo
has just told the story of British cousin Douglas,
how one formal dinner he made the men
rotate one seat clockwise after every course,
the seated women welcoming each new partner,

how the stunned host,

                    stiff old Hans Fenstermacher
hasn't yet closed his mouth…

We laugh, and settle, laugh again, all of us

                             privately
marveling at the fact of vibrant Douglas dead—

                                and then
as if beneath blankets
embroidered with each of our names,

                       we're taken
by the valley's patient quiet…

***

Breeze-blown candles, a twine of smoke, steeples,
then the conversions at dusk…

                    all ineffable,
the promise
of a good night's sleep.

                  Last night, drifting
in bed among the talkative books and poems,
the scent of scotch broom
like incense through the window,

                Stevens
gazed up at me from his papers
like a priest I'd seen lift his head every Sunday
from the homiletic text.

               I can still see
the priest's eyeglasses, so thick
I couldn't stop thinking *he* was the mystery…

***

In college, I imagined the sunset paternal.
Later, I grew skeptical of the heavenly prize

promised in the roseate colors.
                              Like Stevens,
I held to beauty
for its own elaboration,
                    —or tried.
In Italy, what is beautiful
is so
because of the promised world, the waiting friends,
atmospheric proof
of the magic and the redeemed—

how, like the valley, it calls to persuade…

***

In Castelfranco, the evocation of these darkening terraces
is like an errant history
I'm pressed to revise.
                    In the quarter light
of the moonless dusk, not pigeons' song, not distant train,
nothing but fireflies flaring on in airborne silence,
                                        like me,
up here on a mountain, waiting for calm. What I need up here,
alone at the picnic table in my insistent musing,
is old Douglas: Time to rotate, change
the conversation, mix in
a few laughs. I'd like to agree—

But out in the altitudes of the Valdarno,
                              the silence
merely raises an eyebrow, shrugs, says,
I'm at the next chair, then the next,
and
I'll talk about anything, whatever you like…

"Whipping Post"
—1971, 2004

This is his daddy's rock and roll, fast agonistic blues,
my seventeen-year-old flooring the minivan north

through delirium, his West Coast glittering in sunset
road shine. Wind as driver's permit. Wind as muse.

He's smiled for a hundred miles. He's large at the wheel.
You can hear it—it's 9:15 in the Fillmore evening,

New York City, they've got a little number
from their first album they're gonna do for us,

Barry starts it off. Wind as pulse. Wind in road-trip sync.
In twenty-three minutes and three seconds the music

will end. Two minutes later my son will force a pickup
halfway into the left shoulder. The snare ratchet

of stones on the under rig. My shriek as siren.
An adrenaline plume billows in the side window.

My shriek as castrato. That woman in a crosstown bar
made ruin of all our lives, she's tied Gregg

to the whipping post, and these days she's having her way
with him, Duane's guitar sliding sideways. Pretty

fucking great, my son says, parroting the old man.
—And it's come down to this, hasn't it? The whirling

oceanic descent of the bass and organ washing out
both leads, two drummers in a sibilant wind

of cymbals. Three miles up the road the nose of the car
wants to pull right. To lift from the vortex. Sometimes—

and there's Duane's last quick lick—sometimes
Gregg feels like he's almost...like he's almost

dying. This instant, I know we're not the ones to worry,
not yet, it's Duane, dead on a cycle in six months. For now,

there's no need to talk. My son is so in love with his father
that he sends a fist softly into my shoulder, even

as he sings that last verse with Gregg. Up ahead, we're
finally safe in the center lane, elongated instants

collapsed into flesh and blood going north. Fuck death,
I say to myself, —and I punch him back so he hears me.

Flashback at Castelfranco

Dawn in Micanopy, Florida, and the old Impala
Floats the canopy roads, the last hours of acid
Stripping the protective film from the world
So every tree and fence blazes
With end-of-bandwidth jitters, my breath
A shallow tinnitus audible in the orbit
Of my limbs... I cut the radio and slow
To an idle beneath the live oaks, Spanish moss
Dripping to the roadside floor, my only god
The present moment. Then I turn off
The car lights to drift in new moon silence.
For a few seconds, a great maw encloses.
In beauty and terror, I flash the lights back on
To stay true to the road beneath the canopy,
And a white fence glows in a burst
Until I kill the beams again,
One fascination
And another,
The world's first question strobing on and off.

Thirty years later, on this moonless scotch broom hill
Above three sleeping late-Renaissance steeples,
All the little windows flicker on below
Like fireflies in the olive trees.
As the dark mountain hulks beneath the last bright shine
Of sky across the valley, the molecules
Of another air
Seem to flood this one. My ten-year-old
Stands with her binoculars and stares
Into the same alluring Tuscan spill, a silent vista
So redolent one can see how prayer erupts.
Aglow, entranced by sunset, she asks how far
To the mountains, there on the other side.
And as I answer in the explanatory lingua she loves,

A host of paternal lies rise, then resign
In my chest. For I know what she'll come to know
Some long, road-coarse night:
We live in two places at once.
There is darkness and there is the lit-up world,
And behind both
An immeasurable quiet.

This, Then

Every once in a while, it's true: I get sick of dying.
Iambic ghosts choiring
                         their lovely, churchless songs,
All the lines of the poem leaning toward terminus
Like rows of low windbent weeds—

                                        The long vacation laughs
Last summer, Ralph's reed-dry three-beat wise remarks
Fading fast
As I gaze from the first draft,
                              a recognition of the dusk,
The last blaze rose holding to my wife's trellis,
                                        her stone Buddha
Offering its constancy to us,
A hint of musk
Above the blackening daylilies—

***

And so I remind myself of this, then:
                              Not twenty hyaline seconds
After three rattling slams
Shook Aeromexico 448, northbound for LAX,
After the hard starboard lean,
After the thousand foot drop,
                         and the next,
After the screams of the mothers finger-vised to their children,

I knew I'd found the earthbound pivot of the poem. Three days back

As I'd begun writing in San Miguel, where I watched
From the high study window,
                         a single tone
Signaled beyond human ears the instant

The flock of white herons would lift
On a late-morning thermal
                              as if carrying

The old ascending subject

Over the grey and sandstone homes,
The little white Moorish domes mimicking
                                          the sacristies
Of the town's Catholic churches. Between that hilltop window
And the serrated spires of *La Parochia*, the cathedral,
The tall, parched cypress trees
                                 aimed their mortal needs
At an arboreal heaven. As if a message from God
Were tacked on a pennant in the high air, over and over

Every living thing arched skyward—

***

As the pilots say, bad chop is the gut-check.
And yet a week ago the flight south
over the iron-stained desert mountains—
Crossed by that carless road
                              deadheading
Under splotches of cloud shade—
                                  had known only

The airy sentimentality of silk.

When I woke two hours out of LAX
And peered down
At the pearl-white burled base of cloud
And the gnarling tower rising from it,
                              I was home again,
As one is home every few months

Or years
In a recurring dream, the few skittering pre-flight nerves
Quieted, and I remembered
This old version of my escape from death—

How I'd tumble into the lush tropical hold
Of the cloud itself, a bed
In which I'd roll weightless, high over the expanse,

                                                held

In the alert omniscient trance of the poem
Inscribing itself across still blue.

***

We all know, such longing extracts a price.
                                    As it happened,
In that house above San Miguel I began this poem
At a desk beneath the famous Magritte print,
All the black-tied businessmen, validated
In long dark coats and bowlers,
                            —inert, floorless, aloft—
Each briefcase as surreal ballast.
                                Thirty years ago in my journal
I wrote notes for a poem about my sweat-soaked dream of flying,
How I'd soared
            in slow-motion acrobatics
Above the tables, above Ralph and the other drinkers,
Above the bartender and the waitresses
Crowded into some sawdust tavern,
                            happy as gulls
With their lusty crowing, utterly unaware
Of my magic. And, despite my brief weightless joy,

I suddenly knew some clenched maw had spawned the dream—
And, still dreaming,
                alone on the unblanketed sheets,

Ruffled, dank, the twisted splotch of my body
Clawed up the walls of bright falling air—

***

This memory, too, came to me in the seconds
                                    our lives returned.

Like Magritte's floating men,
                    I prefer to hover,
If only with the smile of the momentarily saved—
How did the fear of falling atomize
                            into the air of these lines,
As if I'd been tethered to morphine,
Each drip a dream of flight?
                    A hundred miles
Past the cloud, my wife's grip dammed blood up my arm.
This evening in the garden, when I told her
How the poem's new turn came to me instantly,
                                    how I'd burned
Key lines into memory only moments after the air softened,
She said it was a way
Of riding out the panic in silence, the way
I always deal with dying.

I know: All flights—save one—land safely.
                            Still, for days
After the wind-shear of that storm-dark hammerhead,
I thought I'd worked out a poem
In which a life
Could tear itself from the sky—and then,
                            as if air were art,

    Refuse to fall.

3

The Boat

The sad wooden boat aches in its keelson
to be ruinously drunk, to be something
other, as it drifts out from the averted
shore, too full of its hollow self.
If only to be these rowers, to sweat
as they do in the glaring fog,
to enter the flesh. If only for the sleek fish
to pout and roll up under the bottom
as a cat purls beneath the outstretched legs
of its foolish, grateful master, the widow
with her gray book of services. Then: To be
the widow, just then convinced she sees
through the eye of the smallest particulate
the convex breadth of the first world,
the grasses in sunlight paring cheerfully back
for a path lined by white stones and curling up
over the hill in a parabola of God
and cat's tail.
               If only for more, for moonlight,
to annihilate the stuffed gulch of clouds,
as the moon once did, the young, sleeping boat
at midlake, waking as a man alone
on the frigid road would quickly turn to find
what it was on his shoulder—and then the fear,
realizing it was the delirious photons
of moonlight to which he'd at last opened.
To know that man's same fear
the night his wife could not stop opening
into herself, her taste, the first minute
and the elegant alabaster surprise
of the second, and then her tears and the high
feathered weeping he heard over her breasts
as she entered the third, and then finally

the last human silence of her fourth, and on,
flooding into him....
                              Long ago the young boat
had stirred under the full moon's face, risen
over the mountain, beaming the narrow white walk
over the fearful water. A thick wind rose
in consent. The lake sent each distinct runnel
of itself crosswise through the walk
as the still boat stared—and knew
this was to be the great moment
of staying still. The moment of nothing
mattering. And then...nothing
came of it, no light spilled away
from the perfect hyaline lake
the boat had always imagined.
It wanted to see at the margins
of its own surface not the gunnels, but
the shaped wooden planks, the varnish
giving way to deep streaks
on light, the streaks to terrain,
maps, numbers...finally, itself.
A last memory of planks in the wind.
Then—just the wind.
                              But dawn had turned
the boat out again, lost as a young husband
before the morning his pregnant wife, fast
from the geneticist, stands outside
his open office, offering a pink
or blue rose over the threshold. And so,
of course, tonight the sad boat longs
to be that man, too, not for the moment
when he lays the fool flower across his arms,
nor when he sees in its inward face
two dazzling children skipping the old path,
nor for just after, when he sweeps
the floating woman into the room and they stare

at each other and repeat one name slowly. No.
Rather, for the moment just after that, his wife
leaving, cheery, an abundant red sail
down the hallway, and he, buoyant, certain,
an immaterial empty bowl pressed upon the water.

Scrim

Book to chest, lost in the rogue, silk-white threads of hair, the scented labyrinth,
he sits peering, swimming
touchless
in her body, shaken in the kind of sultry late afternoon air that had never meant
a thing, not even when he'd forsworn heaven

for the plain secrets of water and sky, when he'd woven himself
into the present moment,
ordinary air inciting all the nerve cells of his lungs like some self-made communion.
This is a dream, he tells himself.
Another layer,

he tells himself. But in today's light, right now, when she looks up from her novel,
it's her face as she speaks, it's her presence,
a painless, cool rip
on his skin, a light menthol wind like the onshore breeze last summer
into which he stared, as now,

over the glassy bay. She'd come down
the cliff stairs, said something funny, intimate, then dropped her book
and towel, approached
the faint surf. In those moments before she broke the sheen of soft water
and stroked

a hundred yards into the shifting, buoyant room of her swim, he fell quiet,
and watched her
in her tight suit standing still, all her loveliness curved taut
before him like a mystery
he should see through. There's nothing more than matter, he reminds and reminds,

just material, he reminds, intoning those m-words
like a logician's mantra. But
her form was the other world his body takes to, the maze he can't navigate
from. He'd been caught then
as he is now, again. And so he's split between the unadorned fact

of merely naked matter in which he stands as flesh and bone alone—
and another realm
in which his own body is a radiance, her presence an aperture into a dream
of clues
as recognizable as the coffee table, but ultimately just as mute, proof of something

else. He knows the drill, the tricks, the sleights of hand, how the balmy face
of the world offers itself up to him
like a prayer book in code,
the seductions that find their way into his waking dreams until he's entered
a candlelit cavern

in which *O Magnum Mysterium* rings out from the subatomic interstices
of an unseeable world. His eyes purse as if he's hurt, as if
he's become lost
in the dim currents of—not resignation—but this originary tidal pull toward her...
Even as he sits so still, the sunset

filtered through high clouds and on into the living room, he's swept out into her
while she speaks. Soon enough
she's laughing about the novel,
saying in that sub-rosa voice, it's as if the facts undermine themselves like years
of tap water

carving the runnel in the kitchen sink. He thinks back to the day at bayside:
How she stood so composed
against the swelling water. Her figure rose in his chest. She'd turned
once to meet his gaze, her legs and back
and—just as now—her face

all a testament
to what has become of him, of his mania for tearing away the promising scrim
so the waves and moon would fall like gods,
so he could believe utterly
in himself alone, not this face across a room, this voice purling in the air like faith.

"Le Secret"

—*after Rodin*

I'd just stepped out of The Classical Tradition
When I saw her looking at the two marble-
White hands poised the instant before touching.
I hadn't noticed the column between them yet.
Her beauty was a given, but the discretion
In her gaze drew me like the dark avenues
Of her pleated print skirt. She'd tipped her head
To see something. The palm-high column at once
Joining and separating the right hands? Each one
Glowed near what it couldn't know.
                                    How easy
To imagine those nights we'd lock together,
Sitting up, riding the pre-tremors
As candles flared shadows between us,
Our posture bolt straight as if emanating
From both of us at once, how we'd lift and drop,
Dive for the plummet promised in each iris,
How every finger anticipates the swoon
Beyond first touch.
                    She hadn't seen me.
She slid her weight from left hip to right,
Slowly circled the stand, her skirt circling
Before winding back. Could I be sure her gaze
Was a deep form into which I'd been invited?
When I stole up close to try the scent of her hair,
She didn't once turn her eyes from the hands, but
Slipped her fingers into the spaces between mine.
It was our twentieth anniversary. We'd come for art.

This Morning

When for the first time in a living creature instinct perceived
itself in its own mirror, the whole world took a pace forward...
　　　　　　　　　—*The Phenomenon of Man*
　　　　　　　　　Teilhard de Chardin, S.J.

How can it be? My wife shining from the shower,
Runnels of water necklaced on her shoulders, the border
Of her body traced for seconds

　　　　　　　　　in a thin white glow so bright

The Trib's tragic litanies float forgotten to the sheets
As I squint from the bed.

　　　　　　　Just then, a single backlit bead
Leaps from her silhouette, and, for a lengthening moment,
I'm anticipating

　　　　　what's already arrived—

***

We all know the man my age in a town up north
Wearing the worn clothes I'd have liked.
We all know he's flexed to a desk,

　　　　　　　exiled
In his apartment's sea of stale air, where every book
And utensil, every chair and table
Sit with him in perfect right angles

As the dust grays upon them. He's killed the windows, stripped
The place of mirrors.

　　　　　Sure, there's pretty light
In the trees outside. But fuck the trees, he says to himself—
And he scribbles wizened elegies onto the tablet.

***

56

My wife isn't the answer, exactly. Not yet

In her underwear, layering lotions across her face,
The even lilt of her morning song, her report done,
The office afloat in easy catch-up,
She's happy to forgo
                          the headlines, the airwaves,
Her mock-salacious tune lowering into weekend plans,
                                                                first

The beach, then
The evening's plunge. I admit I still dream of sex

As a near-mystic path leading to something more,
Not an answer so much as—what? transport?

I know it can't last forever,
                          but its lineal beam
Carries us a while on course,
Into the elevated musings of the next morning

Before we're dispersed again onto the broken sea—

***

Some days you can see him, my sad friend up north,
The wallpaper peeling off cracked plaster,
The infinitesimally small, unproveable kernels
                          of a self
Detaching, aimless motes lapping in the air. He's unhinged
From his desk, pouring himself a drink
In the middle of the valley afternoon, dreaming…

A woman has entered the apartment of dappled light and slips down
Upon him for a hundred years like cool salve. When he wakes,
The path from his desk to his bed

Ends amid dry underbrush.

How can it be I once drank bourbon

***

Late into the night in a ruinous tavern in Yolo or Zamora
While a couple of new friends laughed and the natives
Danced to Charlie Price warbling from the juke?
I've never liked whiskey much,

but I thought I liked that woman
Gurgling at the bar in the red-checked cowgirl shirt,
That woman two decades older than I, if a year...

As we danced those several slow numbers, her big buckle
Ground ovals on my denim crotch. I remember
Her strapped breasts lifting higher onto my chest.
And as she sang along with the songs,

I turned my face
From the bar breath of her smile, each note she sang
Cracked like vinyl shards of old LPs.

When the music stopped,
And the particles of her song had piled above our shoes,
We all know what she asked.

—And, it's true, I'm still laced
With guilt for going home with her,
For heading straight home alone,

for not recalling which...

***

Memories return like old books. This week I'm hooked

On de Chardin again for the sheer labyrinth of his fable.
Decades now I've laughed off his lovely theory,
How we, the desert sand, all matter
Are driven by an irreducible gist

58

To the divine—

           Surely the glory of wishful thinking.

So how can it be that I stumbled upon one inerrant path
That led to this path?
Of course, it's not simply the sex. I've returned here
This summer morning, with coffee,
Alone in the garden,

                  remembering my wife's body
An hour ago, not yet dressed, how she crossed the room
To hold me on the bed
For so many light-strewn minutes

                    without consummation—

But with its otherworldly promise: The moment her skirt rustles
Up the beach path in the imminent evening,

                    or we return home, say,
On a mid-fall night from the late movie with friends,

Or from that long-planned dinner in the little garden ristorante,
The gas heaters bearing light across the realm
Like a candle on the night table,

              then, certainly,
In metaphor or dream, in body and hope, once more

—As if it's seen itself—

An immaterial sub-atomic pearl
Will break free
From the furled walls of a distant universe within me—

And, for a day or two, grant rudder to my drift....

The Bedspread at Echo Lake

                                        Later,
After canoeing, after we've entered each other
In clenched, parental silence,
The lake-reflected sunlight catches the white bedspread
We hold aloft
                    too briefly.
                            Riding nothing
But rogue luck, I hold off this old sadness.
In Vermont's gray luster before dawn,
                                    we stretch
The fabric chest-high above the blue blanket, pulled smooth
As the surface of the lake
                        those hours ago
When she woke me to dress while the kids slept.

I can't help it—
I want her touch, the cedar walls, that freshwater quiet—
I want it all to go on, the canoe
                                forever trailing its vee
Toward the little island where the egret
On the high branch held out one snowy sail.
                                    Barely,
She tugs the spread
And I look up from the water.
                            She's there,
On the other side, waiting out my grip,
Giving the taut cloth a second tug, giving me that wry smile,
As if to say, it's morning,
                        there's no better time to make a bed—

And so, in finite unison, we nod, we let go—
                                    a single white wing
Descending as slowly as it can.

4

Accident Alert

[Dexter Gordon's "I'm a Fool to Want You"
plays for 1:23 — then fades out quickly]

It's 2AM, and San Luis sinks in sleep.
My wife, our kids, my friends reach past the edge
of moonlight on the pillow of two worlds:
Each outstretched hand catches, then grips the dream
hard. Me? For a lost minute, I stare down
the blue-white snowscape of the monitor—
and then a single tentative keystroke
starts off the set. Last night, as my wife dozed
on the couch before bed, Dexter Gordon's
sax poured itself into the ballad like
bourbon. The next word uncovers the scene—
then more words shoveling snow off the ground
of the old story: My stroke-bled father's
last moment with me: Fourteen years old.
February 1st, 1965.
Gray ice knobbed like little talismans.
Steps splinter the glossy, fluorescent halls.
Blood-filled test-tubes taped to the hospital
wall. I still don't know what I'll come to know.
He stares up from a fetal curl. Early
in this draft, I'd wanted to remember
the way he took my mother in his arms
for the big nightly clinch in front of us
as he entered the side door after work,
the way he showed me how to bunt, fingers
on the wood bat soft as rosin, the way
he and my brother Glenn ate radishes
with a sloven, wet-lipped zeal, the way
he held a Jack London novel as if
it were a long-lost sacrament, the way
he poured Ballantine into a pilsner
until the foam rose in a precarious

dome each Saturday night before I watched
him Sunday morning, magical lector
speaking the delirium of the scriptures.
Those otherworldly metrics spilled from him
like that deep blue radiance at the edge
of vision when I close my eyes in search
of the poem's next surprise. We all know why
some of these lines are too maudlin to stay.
A month from now I'll cringe, then delete them.
But I need them to learn the whole story.
The scene on the monitor grows grainy
before sharpening on his bloodless face.
Who knew this last tongue-tied talk between us
would fuel all those poems I'd write that first year
of high school—and then these four echoing
decades, each lineated look back
a touchstone marking the gift in his eye.
His lush lyric honed to that period
like a poem funneled down to what-comes-next.
In four days, resigned but hardly ready,
he will die young. In eight days, just back
from the snowbound graveyard, I'll shoot baskets
in our driveway, while, in the living room,
my black-dressed mother wipes and wipes wet rings
off tables, friends mourning his one-liners,
then roaring in actual high-pitched glee.
Bushmills fuels the celebrants, who know
it's their blood-duty to ward off the devil.
Was it Mr. Logan who came outside
to shoot with me, conceding he believed
the immigrant blarney he'd heard about
the devil's taste for fatherless children?
Right then he'd learned what I would: Poetry
is the art of surprising yourself like that—
with your own words. I was surprised again
four months later when Joe Ryan, the jock

priest with the tough Bayonne accent, dropped off
Louie Untermeyer's little copy
of *Robert Frost's Poems* for me. Joe played
quarterback for St. Peter's, late fifties,
then ran a reverse into the clergy,
reading unmercifully Catholic
Flannery O'Connor—then Eliot,
Thomas, and Auden. No one guessed he'd shed
his collar in two decades for little
Louise B. I dated the gift right then:
May 27th, 1965—
the same day the liner notes record that
Dexter Gordon settled onto a stool
in a studio just a few towns east
in upscale Englewood Cliffs, New Jersey.
Like jazz, real poems are accident alerts.
As I read "Home Burial" a first time,
Frost's grief-stricken childless mother near mad,
pianist Barry Harris found his notes,
Dexter inhaled a slow breath, bent slightly
back, closed his eyes, then—once more—leaned into
"I'm a Fool to Want You." I'd have to wait
thirty years to find that song. When my friend
Mary Kay lent me the cd, she said
it was something I had to hear. Of course
she was right, not that an event is "meant"
to happen, though it could not have happened
any other way. But wait, she hasn't met me
yet: I'm exiting the college chapel
for the last time, my father's faith dispersed
like dust motes in thick antebellum air.
And that's what this poem is heading for—
at least that's what I think it wants: open
closure, the kind that improvs its own end-
lessness. But first it needs to feign neatness,
college over, the rush west, the bad poems

like scrub desert we have to cross, the night
of that packed Christmas party when I strode
the beery kitchen to meet a woman
who spoke a language I hadn't heard in years,
a mortal tune beneath the jest and lunge,
her talk tethered to a template, a map
that takes us back to move us forward.
My father throws high flies outside our home
until dusk comes, until he and the ball
fade. Years on, he and that ball arrive
in my first book, side by side with our kids.
Soon Mary Kay laughs at how I *needed*
my faithlessness. Now she too shows up here.
It's true: *Good* accidents invent themselves
with stylized, indifferent whimsy,
as if the Big Bang authored them as fate
we ignore or exploit. My wife gets up
from bed, 3AM, you really should sleep,
she warns, or the poem will abandon you.
Lucky poems marry themselves to the brief
pulse of the world as it goes by.
Okay, she's right, soon I *will* head to bed.
But not yet. The poem doesn't want to go
where it knows it must: Twenty-one years ago,
I enter the house, and she looks at me,
sax decrescending—Joe's dead in Jersey,
49, sitting in a chair, Louise
out shopping with the baby, a book
fallen to the floor. I never did learn
the title. At the grave, a priest chanted.
I stared off at the snow under the clouds,
its shimmering, sunless blue radiance...
To think now of that name, so romantic,
on the cd cover: *Blue Note.* How long
—maybe three minutes?—has Dexter led us
away, down his breathy tributaries.

We haven't noticed the existential figure
in the dark corner of the studio.
Remember: I'm fifteen now, and the wife
in "Home Burial" lashes her husband
with cold grief because he could bury *him*,
their dead child, as if, she thinks, it wasn't
any different from ordinary work.
Freddy Hubbard hasn't played a note yet.
My mother sleeps. I'm transfixed in the poem
while the trumpeter glides up to the mike,
Dexter's sax gives way to Freddy's horn,
lifting like a parallel world, a dream
in which a woman is always walking
away from a man: It's Dexter; the fool
still wants her, but Freddy knows the truth
Dexter just can't face yet: She'll never
return, the moment's past—but then it's more
than that, the child still leaving the mother,
Freddy's one-minute solo playing on,
then he too leaves like the gods, my father
gone. Then it's Joe. Even my wife is lost
in her dreams. That's when Dexter returns,
lips pursed dark blue, ready to fight for her,
until he knows what he's known all along—
we're on our own. But since he's alive
and alone under the single spotlight
that chiaroscuros the stage into night
and snow, he'll acknowledge Freddy's solo
as if nothing could ever happen next—
And it all goes down like this: One, two, three…

[*"I'm a Fool to Want You" fades in from 2:53 to finish*]

Notes

"Eight Hours in the Nixon Era": Early on November 18th, 1973 Richard Nixon flew to Key Biscayne, Florida, after having had a press conference the previous day in which he proclaimed: "I am not a crook."

"James Dickey at Florida": "The Performance," "Falling," and "Cherry Log Road" in *The Whole Motion: Collected Poems, 1945-1992* by James Dickey. *Also The World as a Lie: James Dickey* by Henry Hart, pp 523-24.

"Self-Portrait with Expletives": A "stunting linebacker" is a defensive football player who doesn't rush the quarterback directly but tries to deceive the offensive players by crossing in front of or behind a fellow defensive player. A player is "clotheslined" when he is tackled by being hit suddenly from the neck up.

"Radio Fate": *Wanda Hickey's Night of Golden Memories: And Other Disasters* and *In God We Trust: All Others Pay Cash*, both by Jean Shepherd.

"Solstice Over the Valdarno": The epigraph comes from "Sea Surface Full of Clouds" by Wallace Stevens.

"'Whipping Post'": *The Allman Brothers at Fillmore East*, originally recorded by The Allman Brothers Band in 1971, six months before Duane Allman was killed in a motorcycle accident.

"This, Then": The Magritte painting is *Gonconda* (1953). "Bad chop" refers to rough, in-flight turbulence.

"Scrim": "O Magnum Mysterium" is a centuries-old, responsorial Christmas chant celebrating the birth of Christ.

"'Le Secret'": Rodin's marble sculpture (1909) of this name.

"This Morning": *The Phenomenon of Man* by Teilhard de Chardin.

"Accident Alert": *Clubhouse* by Dexter Gordon, with Freddy Hubbard, Barry Harris, Bob Cranshaw, Ben Tucker, and Billy Higgins (Blue Note Records, 2006; originally recorded 1965).

THE LENA-MILES WEVER TODD POETRY SERIES

The editors and directors of the Lena-Miles Wever Todd Poetry Series select one book of poems for publication by Pleiades Press and Winthrop University each year. All selections are made blind to authorship in an open competition for which any American poet is eligible.

OTHER BOOKS IN THE SERIES

Pacific Shooter by Susan Parr
(selected by Susan Mitchell)

It was a terrible cloud at twilight by Alessandra Lynch
(selected by James Richardson)

Compulsions of Silkworms and Bees by Julianna Baggott
(selected by Linda Bierds)

Snow House by Brian Swann
(selected by John Koethe)

Motherhouse by Kathleen Jesme
(selected by Thylias Moss)

Lure by Nils Michals
(selected by Judy Jordan)

The Green Girls by John Blair
(selected by Cornelius Eady)

A Sacrificial Zinc by Matthew Cooperman
(selected by Susan Ludvigson)

The Light in Our Houses by Al Maginnes
(selected by Betty Adcock)

Strange Wood by Kevin Prufer
(selected by Andrea Hollander Budy)